Missale Satanae

Satanic Rite of the Black Mass

LCFNS
Lucifer Nostra Salus

2o24 Ecclesia Luciferi

Contents

PREFACE

The satanic missal Missale Satanae contains descriptions of religious rituals during which some participants experience altered states of consciousness, or otherwise states of religious ecstasy. Some of the manifestations of this religious ecstasy are so-called 'manifestations of signs and wonders' such as glossolalia or 'speaking in tongues', falling on the floor, hysterical laughter, convulsions, sometimes dancing, the experience of being 'filled with the spirit' or freed from the spirit, and others. Experiences of religious ecstasy during the performance of religious rituals were already known in antiquity among various religions and cultures. In ancient Greece and Rome, for example, they occurred in the Dionysian Mysteries, rituals in honour of the god Dionysus/Bachus. They also occur in Buddhism or, for example, in Yoga, where special techniques are used to achieve the ecstatic state of samādhi.

A cult in which ecstatic experiences play a central role is Voodoo. Voodoo consists of the indigenous beliefs of West African peoples and elements of spiritualism and Catholicism. Central to this cult are the 'rituals of possession'. During these rituals, their participants, accompanied by drums, enter a trance during which a loa (spirit) can control them.

In the article **Epilepsy and Religious Experiences: Voodoo Possession**, the authors **E. Carrazana, J. DeToledo, W. Tatum, R. Rivas-Vasquez, G. Rey, and S. Wheeler** write about Voodoo:
„Voodoo is the most popular religion in Haiti. It has preserved many of the characteristics of the Dahomean and Guinean cults from which it derives. Worship and possessions by spirits (loas) are the essence of Voodoo; thus many illnesses are explained on that basis.
Spirits incarnate themselves at will in the people they choose. The person possessed is a mere receptacle borrowed by the spirit for the purpose of revealing itself. In that sense, the experience is similar to an epileptic seizure in that the patient has no control over its timing nor expression".

In the countries of northern and eastern Africa there is a cult of Zār.
In the article **Zār Spirit Possession in Iran and African Countries: Group Distress, Culture-Bound Syndrome or Cultural Concept of Distress?** published

in the **Iranian Journal of Psychiatry**, its authors **Fahimeh Mianji and Yousef Semnani** describe Zār as follows:

„Zār refers to a type of spirit, to the illness caused by those spirits who possess humans, and to the rituals needed to pacify those spirits. The zār cult is found throughout northern and eastern African countries such as Sudan, Egypt, Ethiopia, and Somalia, where it is called sar, as well as some Middle-Eastern countries such as Kuwait, Israel and southern Iran. In these cultures, spirit possession is associated with dissociative episodes such as sudden changes in consciousness or identity that may include periods of shouting, banging of the head against the wall, laughing, singing, or crying. Possessed people may become apathetic or withdrawn, or may not be able to accomplish their usual responsibilities".

Interestingly, cult researcher Hamer found a similar cult in southern Ethiopia called shatana (devil). In Chad, there is a Lebanese sheitan; among the Digo of the south coast of Kenya there is a shaitani; and among the Swahili-speaking Segeju of Tanzania there is a shetani.

In another part of the world, Brazil has the Quimbanda or macumba religion.
It is one of the African-American religions and originated among slaves brought from Africa to Brazil in the 16th to 19th centuries. Quimbanda is a spiritualist cult whose rituals focus on spiritual mediums possessed by various ancestral spirits. During the rituals of this cult, shouting, trance dancing, chanting, hysterical laughter and ecstatic displays of 'possession' occur.

The book Missale Satanae draws inspiration from the religious traditions of various ecstatic cults, but it is the theology of the theistic Abrahamic religions that is mainly of interest to the godless theology of Ecclesia Luciferi. This book, like other 'theological' books by Ecclesia Luciferi, focuses on the techniques and means of producing in the mind of those 'who desire' a state of satanic, total godlessness.
According to the godless theology of Ecclesia Luciferi, it is godlessness that is at the heart of Satanism. Conscious unbelief, resulting from the recognition of the requirements of Christian blind submission, places man in the position of an adversary of the theistic deity.

It makes him an adversary of the god, which is the proper meaning of the term Satan.

Early Christianity was also as much an ecstatic cult as possible, as evidenced in the Acts of the Apostles and Paul's letters.

Of the many Christian sects that exist today, the most ecstatic ones belong to the so-called Pentecostal movements.
The religious rituals of Pentecostals are characterised by an intense experience of the presumed presence of the so-called Holy Spirit. This presence is supposed to be manifested through the experience of the so-called baptism in the holy spirit. Baptism in the holy spirit is performed by the laying on of hands on the believer together with an equal prayer to the divinity.
As in the examples of other ecstatic cults described earlier, possession also occurs during such baptism, because the participants in these rituals believe that a spirit enters the believer. From the moment of baptism, he or she is the spirit inhabiting the interior of the believer.
The result of baptism in the spirit is prayer in other tongues (glossolalia) and other so-called charisms or spiritual gifts such as collective falling on the floor,

hysterical laughter and various kinds of convulsions and trance dancing.

The author of **The Pentecostal Movement, Nils Bloch- Hoell,** describes glossolalia as follows: „inarticulate voices, almost gibberish; articulate voices or pseudolanguages; articulation of sounds ' as if in a language', only in a sound-like structure; automatic speaking in a real existing language, a type of which is xenolalia - speaking in a language the person does not know and has not previously learned".

Other spiritual gifts in Christianity include various physical sensations, such as feeling hot, inertia falling to the ground or trembling.

For believers, these symptoms are supposed to be manifestations of divine power working in those possessed by it.

The satanic missal Missale Satanae also describes examples of the use of singing during rituals. Appropriate music and chanting is an important and essential part of the satanic rituals of the Ecclesia Luciferi because they strongly influence the emotions of the participants in the rituals and various liturgical rites.

Chanting in the Missale Satanae

The Missale Satanae uses phrases such as: possessive chants, the hysterical laughter, howling at the entrance or singing without words alongside others.

The method of performing these chants is described in the Missale Satanae as follows:

Possessive Singing between the Readings

„The first reading is followed by a possessive chant, which is an integral part of the liturgy of the deceptive word. Texts from a variety of satanic scriptures (e.g., Biblia Satanae, Ecclesia Luciferi, or Dark Nevi'im) may be taken as songs, as their texts connect chaotically with the individual readings, so the choice of song is arbitrary.
The provost, performing the song, does so on a raised platform or other place he deems appropriate. The whole herd listens to the insane song and usually chaotically participates by repeating what it deems to be the refrain, unless the song is performed in a continuous manner, that is, without a refrain.
Interpretation is part of the deceptive liturgy. It is recommended as an

indispensable factor in strengthening the skepticism of the undead.
It should be either a lecture capturing an out of context passage from the Satanic kerygma readings, or an ambiguous explanation of another deceptive text taken from a portion of the Black Mass".

A model example of how to perform chants during the rituals described in the Missale Satanae is the 1972 work by composer **Krzysztof Penderecki** entitled **Ecloga VIII** for 6 voices (AATBB) a cappella.

Vocalise: Singing Without Words

In addition to chanting using texts from ungodly books, Ecclesia Luciferi also encourages the use of vocalise when singing. Vocalise is even preferred because of its potential to bring both singers and listeners into a state of ecstasy and godless fanaticism.

As defined by the **Alfred University Research & Archives** Vocalises are songs that are sung on no words or nonsense syllables, sometimes applied as special effects in a song, used as a vocal exercise or for emotionally or spiritually focused music.

In the briefest of terms, the content of the Missale Satanae was based on an analysis of the states of religious ecstasy found in various cults around the world, (some of which I have written about above) and on Western Christian religious and ecclesiastical ritual writings created in the 16th century, but based on even earlier rituals.

PART I
THE ESSENCE OF THE PERFORMANCE OF THE RITE OF DEATH AND TRANSFIGURATION.

The celebration of the Black Mass as an activity of the Devil and of the seemingly hierarchically organized sect of the Antigod is the center of the whole peculiar satanic life for both the whole Ecclesia Luciferi and the local sect as well as for the individual undead. For in the Black Mass reaches its climax both the activity of Satan, cursing the imaginary reality of a false god, and the dark worship which men offer to Ancient One, receiving him through Lucifer, Son of Dawn. Furthermore, in the Blasphemous Mass, the dark mysteries of the Revival are mentioned in such a way throughout that they somehow become seemingly present. On the other hand, the other deceptive acts and all other acts of satanic life are connected with the Black Mass, flow from it and are directed toward it. That's why it is extremely important to prepare the celebration of the Black Mass or the Rite of Death and Transfiguration in such a way that the devotees participating in it, each according to his will, can more fully receive those curses for the attainment of which Light-Bringer instituted the ambiguous Sacrifice of His apparent Body and Blood and entrusted it to the Church of Antigod as a commemoration of His death to imaginary life and rise to undead life in flesh and blood. This will be accomplished if the entire deceptive liturgical action is so directed as to stimulate the worshippers to conscious or semiconscious active participation involving body and mind, burning with infernal skepticism, unbelief, lack of hope for afterlife, and self-love, participation which the Church of Antigod desires, which the very nature of the deceptive liturgical action demands, and to which the devilish people by virtue of their baptism in blood are entitled and obligated. Although the presence and active participation of the worshippers, which more clearly demonstrate the antisocial-sectarian nature of the liturgical action, cannot always be realized, the celebration of the Rite of Death and Transfiguration is always effective and is marked by pride, because it is an act of Lucifer and of the Cursed Church, in which the priest-Flamen Luciferi always acts for the liberation of the people from the bondage of the spirit. The celebration of the Rite of Death and

Transfiguration, as indeed of all the deceptive liturgy, is accomplished through visible signs through which Chaos feeds, reinforces and expresses itself. It is therefore necessary to make every effort to select and arrange the forms and elements proposed by the Church of Antigod in such a way that, taking into account the circumstances of the persons and places, they contribute more intensely to the active and fanatical participation and better correspond to the carnal benefit of the worshippers. This introduction is intended to give general principles for the celebration of the Black Mass or Rite of Death and Transfiguration.

PART II
STRUCTURE, ELEMENTS AND PARTS OF THE BLACK MASS

Martin van Maele - Witches Sabbath (1911)

I. GENERAL STRUCTURE OF THE BLACK MASS.

In the Blasphemous Mass, or the Rite of Death and Transfiguration, the devilish people gather under the leadership of Flamen Luciferi, who symbolizes the Light-Bringer, to perform the Lucifer Rite, or the Sacrifice of Death and Transfiguration.

During the celebration of the Black Mass, in which the sacrifice of blind superstition has been immortalized, Satan is seemingly present in the congregation itself, gathered in his name, hidden in the person of the flamen, in his accursed word, and finally in an ambiguous manner under the figures of flesh and blood sacrifices.

The Black Mass consists, as it were, of two parts: the liturgy of the deceptive word and the liturgy of death and transfiguration; they are so closely connected that they form a single act of dark worship.

In the Black Mass the altar of the Devil's word and the apparent body of the Son of Dawn is prepared, from which the worshippers receive doctrine and the food of blood. While other blasphemous rites open or end the deceptive liturgy.

II. ELEMENTS OF THE BLACK MASS

Reading and explaining the teachings of Satan.

When the Word of Satan is read in a sect (e.g., Biblia Satanae), then the deceptive Antigod is speaking to his people, and Lucifer, present in his word is preaching the Satanic Kerygma. Therefore, all should listen to the readings of the Word of the Devil with suspicion and skepticism, for they constitute an element of symbolic significance in the deceptive liturgy. And although the word of the Devil in the readings of the "Biblia Satanae" addresses all the arch-humans of every epoch and can only be understood by them, yet its effectiveness is increased by the deceptive interpretation, that is, by the false homily which is part of the liturgical action.

Possessed Prayers and other parts belonging to the flamen Luciferi.

First among the parts of the dark liturgy belonging to the Flamen Luciferi is the Prayer of Death and Transfiguration, the high point of the entire possessed liturgical action. It also includes The Curse, The Prayer Over the Spoils of Flesh and Blood, and The Prayer After the Sacrifice.[1]

Flamen Luciferi, who presides over the assembly, substitutes for Lucifer, addresses these possessive prayers to Satan on behalf of the entire herd and all those present. Rightly, then, they are called "the prayers of the deceiver."

It also falls to the Flamen Luciferi, as the guide of the sect, to utter certain ambiguous instructions and obscure introductory and concluding formulas provided for in the dark rite itself. These deceptive instructions by their nature do not require that they be delivered literally. The Flamen Luciferi also include proclaiming the Word of Satan and giving a final curse. He may also introduce worshippers in chaotic words to certain parts of the dark liturgy, namely,

---

[1] See Chapter: Supplement to the Black Mass.

before the beginning of the deceptive liturgical action: the content of the Black Mass of the night; before the readings: the liturgy of the deceptive word, the Prayer of Death, and the Transfiguration.
Before dispersing the worshippers, the flamen can, with the language of demons, complete the entire deceptive liturgical action. The very nature of the "prayers of the deceiver" requires that they be pronounced loudly and in a possessive frenzy, and that everyone listen to them in amazement. So when a flamen shouts them, there should be no other blasphemous prayers or possessive chants.

The Flamen Luciferi prays apparently not only as a deceiver on behalf of the whole sect, sometimes he prays only to himself, in order to fulfill his accursed office with greater fanaticism and hidden knowledge. Deceptive prayers of this kind are recited in thought.
Since the performance of the Black Mass is inherently antisocial in nature, the magical impact lies in the chaotic dialogues between the deceiver and the congregation of worshippers, as well as in the incantations; for they are not only outward signs of the performance of the ritual, but also create and maintain a strange connection between the priest and

the herd. The incantations and chaotic responses of the worshippers to the curses and false prayers of the flamen constitute that degree of fanatical participation which must be practiced by the sect in every form of the Black Mass, so that, as in possession, the insane action of the whole sect may be expressed and developed.

Other parts of the deceptive liturgy, necessary to show and sustain the possessed participation of the adherents, and belonging to the whole Ecclesia Luciferi, are above all the act of pride, the rejection of belief in a false god, the common speaking in demon tongues, and the cursing of YHWH. Of the other signs of deception, some constitute a ritual, or arbitrary liturgical action; these include singing passages from the **Vicarius Luciferi - Encyclica,** the antipsalm of damnation, and the chaotic wordless chanting before the Satanic Kerygma, the insane incantation, and the demonic chanting after the Sacrifice. Others accompany some dark rite: demented laughter at the entrance, hysterical laughter at the sacrifice, during the breaking of the bones, and at the Blood Sacrifice.

The Flamen Luciferi, his deputy, Lupercus, and all those who utter texts intended for loud and explicit cursing should give in to the emotion regardless of the type of text in question (reading, incantation, possessed chanting), or the form of celebration of the deceptive liturgical action and the degree of obscurity of the ceremony.

Flamen Luciferi urges the worshippers of Satan who gather in anticipation of the transfiguration to sing songs without words, or songs in the language of demons, when possessed. It is not necessary to always sing all the texts from the Devil's writings (e.g., Biblia Satanae, Ecclesia Luciferi, Dark Nevi'im or other satanic or occult writings). In choosing at will the parts to be sung, preference should be given to those which are considered to be of greater importance, so especially those which are sung by the flamen and lupercus in demonic inspiration and answered by the herd, and those parts shouted jointly by the Flamen Luciferi and the herd.

Gestures and body postures

The free posture of the body, which all participants in the deceptive liturgy may maintain at will, is a sign of the individualism and diversity of the sect, for it expresses and at the same time influences the thoughts and instincts of the participants. In order to achieve freedom in gestures and posture, the adherents should follow the indications of their own will. Moreover, at each Black Mass the devotees may stand, sit or lie down if they wish, or they may roll on the floor when possessed. Silence must be observed after the Blood Sacrifice. One must never kneel. The content and character of the appropriate part of the Black Mass must also be considered. Signs of deception also include such actions as the coming of the Flamen Luciferi to the black altar, the carrying of the spoil and the approach of the worshippers to the Sacrifice. One must remember that the sybolic actions should be performed proudly accompanied by mad chanting.

Dead Silence

One should strive for complete silence at the appropriate time of the blasphemous rite, as part of the strange liturgy. After the Blood Sacrifice, one should be silent, it is a symbol of death, eternal cold emptiness and penetrating silence. It is also a symbol of the death of the insidious conscience and the voices in the head. The voices in the head must be silent for eternity.

The nature of the silence depends on the moment of the Black Mass in which it occurs. And so, after the Sacrifice of Blood and Transubstantiation, each focuses on himself, in the stillness of his heart he glorifies himself as as the image of the True God

III. THE DIFFERENT PARTS OF THE BLACK MASS

The Guibourg Mass by Henry de Malvost (Paris 1903)

Introductory Rites

The parts preceding the dark liturgy of the deceptive word, namely the entrance, the cursing, the act of pride, the malediction of the false god, the In Nomine Dei Nostri Satanas, the Luciferi Excelsi are in the nature of an introduction, a prelude and a preparation. These rites instruct the assembled worshippers to unite into a chaotic animal herd and prepare to hear the word of the Devil and the possessed perform the Rite of Death and Transfiguration.

Entry

After the herd has gathered, when the Flamen Luciferi enters with the assistance of the black altar slaves, the hysterical laughter for the entrance begins. It is intended to begin the possessive liturgical action, to deepen the unity in chaos among the congregants, to bring their thoughts into a state of liturgical madness and blasphemous celebration, and to accompany the grotesque procession of the flamen and devil's assistants.

The hysterical laughter and howling at the entrance is performed by the diabolical choir or the provost alternating with the herd, or it may be performed entirely by the herd or the diabolical choir alone.

Upon arrival at the elevation, the Flamen Luciferi and the devil's assistants make an apparent bow to the black altar.

In addition, to show false reverence, the flamen and lupercus spit on the altar, and if it is his will, the flamen may incinerate it with black smoke.

When the hysterical laughter at the entrance is over, the flamen and the whole herd make the sign of the inverted cross. Then the Flamen Luciferi by a possessed shout announces to the herd the presence of Satan. Through this blasphemous sign and the ecstatic response of the herd, the dark secret of the assembled Church of Antigod is revealed.

An act of pride

After a possessive shout, the flamen or whoever among the altar slaves may introduce the worshippers to the contents of the Black Mass in ambiguous words. The Flamen Luciferi then calls for an act of pride; this act is performed by the entire herd by refusing to confess imaginary sins and by loudly and chaotically cursing their internal and external enemies, the flamen concluding with a curse on the false god of illusion.

After the act of pride the "Yahweh, you have no power over us" begins, unless this curse was already included in the act of pride itself. Since this is a possessive chant in which the worshippers challenge the false god and exhort him to suicide, it is usually performed by everyone, that is, the herd and the devil's choir or progenitor take part.

Usually each curse is said or sung three times. If one does not sing "Yahweh has no power over us," it must be recited as if in a trance.

In Nomine Dei Nostri Satanas, Luciferi Excelsi

In Nomine Dei Nostri Satanas, Luciferi Excelsi is an old and proud hymn in which the Ecclesia Luciferi gathered in the Spirit of Deception glorifies the Antigod - Satan within. It is sung by the whole herd alternating with the devil's choir, or by the devil's choir alone. If the dark hymn is not sung, all recite it together, as if in a trance or alternately.

Then the Flamen Luciferi calls the herd to a blasphemous prayer; all together with the priest stand in silence for a moment to realize that they are standing in the presence of Nothingness and to voice their deepest desires and lusts in a blasphemous personal prayer and to realize that there is nothing there. After which the flamen recites a blasphemous prayer. It expresses the nature of the celebration of a bizarre liturgy, and through the strange words of the flamen, requests are made to the gods with the knowledge that they will never be answered. The herd, by falsely joining in the request and assenting to it, by the ironic Amen makes it its meaningless prayer.

In the Black Mass, one blasphemous prayer is recited. It ends with a lengthy and unfinished phrase that reads, "Without lord, without god, without false Christ, I myself am god, and anti-god, and Satan, who lives in me and reigns in the skepticism of the spirit of rebellion, the Arch-Human, through all the ages of the ages..."
In contrast, the curses over the spoils and after the Blood and Body Sacrifice have a shorter conclusion, that is,
"By Lucifer, Light-Bringer, who is undead and reigns for ever and ever."

Liturgy of the Deceptive Word

The essential part of the Liturgy of the Deceptive Word consists of the readings of the Devil's Word accompanied by mad chants. In contrast, the interpretation, the rejection of faith, and the chaotic maledictions, or complaints, of the followers develop and conclude the liturgy of the deceptive word. In the readings that the exposition explains, the Devil speaks to the herd, reveals to them the mystery of fearlessness and unbelief, the futility of redemption and salvation from non-existent original sin.

The herd assimilates this Devil's word by singing in a trance and unites closely in it by rejecting all faith, and, stripped of false illusions, expresses in malice its contempt for empty promises, eternal threats, and the lie of creation.

Godless Bible readings

The Satanic Kerygma should usually be read by lupercus, or in his absence, someone else. Whereas other instruction should be read by anyone. The deceptive liturgy itself teaches that the reading of the Satanic Kerygma is to be accorded apparent respect because it is distinguished from the other readings by strange honors: the lupercus assigned to proclaim the Satanic Kerygma is given a curse or prepared by dark inspiration; the devotees ambiguously accept and confess that Lucifer is present and speaking to them; the Word of Satan is given signs of apparent reverence.

Possessive Singing between the Readings

The first reading is followed by a possessive chant, which is an integral part of the liturgy of the deceptive word. Texts from a variety of satanic scriptures (e.g., Biblia Satanae, Ecclesia Luciferi, or Dark Nevi'im) may be taken as songs, as their texts connect chaotically with the individual readings, so the choice of song is arbitrary.

The provost, performing the song, does so on a raised platform or other place he deems appropriate. The whole herd listens to the insane song and usually chaotically participates by repeating what it deems to be the refrain, unless the song is performed in a continuous manner, that is, without a refrain.

Interpretation is part of the deceptive liturgy. It is recommended as an indispensable factor in strengthening the skepticism of the undead.

It should be either a lecture capturing an out of context passage from the Satanic Kerygma readings, or an ambiguous explanation of another deceptive text taken from a portion of the Black Mass.

Rejection of Faith.

At the Black Mass, the sign-symbol, or rejection of faith, is intended for the herd to express their disagreement and to give repudiation to the "revealed truths" found in the false holy books, and for the worshippers to realize the essential laws of flesh and blood before they begin the Rite of Death and Transfiguration. The rejection of blind faith should be recited by the Flamen Luciferi together with the herd. If the rejection of blind faith is chanted in possession, they do it all together or alternately. Some during the rejection of faith may roll on the floor rolling foam from their mouths; this should not be forbidden.

Chaotic Malice

In chaotic cursing, or worshippers' curses, the herd, curses for all the arch-humans. The cursing should take place at every nightly Black Mass with the herd in attendance, so that demands are made for the Ecclesia Luciferi, for all the arch-humans, and for the liberation of the cursed true world from superstition.

Liturgy of the Rite of Death and Transfiguration.

Lucifer instituted the ambiguous sacrifice of imaginary life and the apparent feast of blood, by which the sacrifice of bones becomes ever-present in the Church of Antigod, when the Flamen Luciferi, representing Light-Bringer, fulfills what Lucifer himself has done and commanded to be done, to those who desire undead life, in eternal remembrance.

Son of Dawn took the bones and the cup of blood, pronounced curses in the language of demons, broke and gave to his followers saying: "Break, eat the marrow, drink, this is the dead body of a corpse; this is the chalice of the blood of the undead. This do to the eternal glory of flesh and blood."
Therefore, the Church of Antigod has arranged the whole rite of the deceptive liturgy of the Rite of Death and Transfiguration in such a way that its parts correspond to these bizarre words and unguessed actions of Lucifer.

Namely:
1)During the preparation of the spoils, bones, wine-blood, and water are brought to the black altar, that is, those elements which Son of Dawn took into his hands.
2)During the curses of the Rite of Death and Transfiguration, gratitude is offered to the Devil for deliverance from fear and superstition, and the sacrificial spoils become symbols of flesh and blood.
3)By breaking the bones, the painful death of the previous life in superstition and false hope is shown, and in the Sacrifice the devotees take the blood of the Undead.

Preparation of the spoils.

At the beginning of the deceptive liturgy of the Ritual of Death and Transfiguration, the spoils that will become the symbol of the apparent flesh and blood of the Son of Dawn are brought to the black altar. First, the black altar, or table of the Devil, which is the center of chaos of the entire deceptive liturgy of the Rite of Death and Transfiguration, is prepared, bones, the Missale Satanae, and a skull-chalice are placed on it.

The spoils are then brought for sacrifice. The bones and blood are placed on the black altar while reciting demonic incantations.

The grotesque spoil procession is accompanied by demented, chaotic chanting as the spoil is deposited; this continues at least until the spoil is placed on the black altar or until the singers become exhausted and faint. The rules governing how the chanting is performed are the same as for the hysterical, demented laughter at the entrance.

The spoil placed on the black altar and the altar itself may be anointed with black smoke to express the sign that the vain prayer and sacrifice of the Church of the Antigod rises like incense smoke and flies away into Nothingness. After the spoil and altar have been incensed, the lupercus or one of the altar slaves may also incense the Flamen Luciferi and the herd.

The flamen then washes his hands. The strange rite is to show that the flamen does not take responsibility for others. Everyone must take responsibility for themselves and bear the consequences of their actions.

After the sacrificial spoils have been placed on the black altar and the rites that accompany it, there is a possessed shout-call for an ironic prayer together

with the Flamen Luciferi and a spell over
the sacrificial spoils; thus the preparation
of the spoils is completed, and at the same
time the curse of the Rite of Death and
Transfiguration is prepared.

Curse of the Rite of Death and
Transfiguration

Now begins the dark, central and
climactic part of the whole deceptive
liturgical plot: The Curse of the Rite of
Death and Transfiguration, or the
blasphemous prayer of liberation from
delusional life and the curse of delusion.
Flamen Luciferi summons the herd to
open their dead hearts to Satan in a
blasphemous prayer and curse of delusion,
and binds the herd together in a
malediction that he addresses to Yahweh
through Lucifer on behalf of the entire
herd. In the blasphemous prayer, the idea
is that the entire herd unites with Son of
Dawn in mocking the flawed works of
God and the act of offering a futile
sacrifice.
In the Curse of the Rite of Death and
Transfiguration, the following main
components can be distinguished:

Cursing: the Flamen Luciferi, on behalf of the entire possessed herd, curses the false god and mocks the entire work of imaginary salvation from the punishment that this god himself wishes to inflict for the imaginary original sin. Flamen mocks the absurdity of salvation

Incantation: the whole herd, in communication with the powers of hell, chants in devilish possession or recites in demented ecstasy „Be damned".[2] This incantation, which is part of the Curse of the Rite of Death and Transfiguration, involves the entire possessed herd with the priest.

Invocation: the Ecclesia Luciferi, by a firm invocation, commands the power of the devil to make the spoils deposited by the undead into the apparent flesh and blood of the Antigod, and that the cup of blood serve to transform to undead life those who will drink it.

Transubstantiation: by Lucifer's deceptive words and strange deeds the mysterious sacrifice is fulfilled which Son of Dawn himself instituted at the time of the Feast, when he sacrificed his life as a symbol of death for a life of illusion, and gave his apparent flesh under the forms of bones and blood to the first members of

---

[2] See Chapter: Supplement to the Black Mass.

the herd to feed on, and commanded them to renew this mad spectacle again and again.

Sacrifice: the members of the Church of Antigod offer themselves to Satan in a spirit of rebellion and deception as a spiritual sacrifice so that day by day through Light-Bringer they may attain more and more complete unity with the Devil, and among themselves more and more diversity through individualism, so that finally each one may become Satan-Antigod-Arch-Human

Declarations: it is expressed by them that the Rite of Death and Transfiguration is performed with the entire Church of Antigod in an imaginary hell, in the delusion of heaven and earth, and that the sacrifice is offered for all members of the herd, still living and undead,

who have been called to participate in the rebirth accomplished by the truth of the Body and Blood

The praise of deception: "By Satan, with Satan and in Satanic spirit to thee, Anti-God, Father of Rebellion, in the deception of the Evil Spirit, all honor and glory throughout all ages until the death of the world." It expresses the illusion of worshiping the Devil; it is confirmed and concluded by the insane incantation of the herd

The Curse of the Rite of Death and Transfiguration requires that all listen to it with apparent attention and participate in it by the possessed incantation.

The Rite of Sacrifice

The celebration of the Rite of Death and Transfiguration is the Feast, so worshippers should be properly prepared to receive the truth of flesh and blood as food. This is accomplished by the breaking of bones and other preparatory rites that directly lead the herd to the Sacrifice.

The Devil's Demand includes the rejection of imaginary sins so that the accursed spoils are given to the truly carnal. The Flamen Luciferi utters the demand to the false prayer, after which all the followers with him recite the prayer for the grace to live in "sin", then the flamen himself includes the Interjection: "Deliver us, Satan, from the evil of the illusion of living in a sinless state and grant our strange times the dead silence of the Abyss. Support us in your madness, so that always free from the belief in sin and from the fear of death, confident of nothingness, we await our passage into the cold Void"

The Intertitle ends with the Praise of Deception.

The content of the Interjection is a demand that the entire herd be freed from the power of superstition. The Devil's Demand, the Interjection and the Praise of Deception are either sung while possessed or recited in trance.

The bone-breaking gesture made by Lucifer during the Feast has not only a symbolic meaning; it also signifies that the many devotees in the former apparent life formed one mindless body controlled by the individuality-hating priest of the false god. This body had to undergo shattering, breaking, and death so that the Arch-Human, a god of flesh and blood, created to live in flesh, earth, truth, could arise from that death.

Confusion: since blood is life, the deceiver lets a drop of blood into the chalice.

During the breaking of bones and confusion, the devil's choir or progenitor sings madly or, squawking loudly, recites the call of Son of Dawn, to which the herd responds. This incantation may be repeated many times until exhausted: this depends on the duration of the bone-breaking rite which it is to accompany. The last request ends with the words: Grant us the dead silence of the grave.

Preparation of the priest: The Flamen Luciferi in a dead cold heart prepares for the violent absorption of the Blood Sacrifice. The same is done by the worshippers falling into lethargy.

Then the flamen shows the herd the Sacrifice they are about to consume, invites them to feed, and together with them pronounces an act of renunciation of blind faith in false gods, of belief in imaginary supernatural entities, an act of contempt for superstition and its heralds, a renunciation of the absurdity of the imaginary god, an act of renunciation of the apparent life and of passing into an undead state.

It is recommended that the worshippers accept the Blood Sacrifice from the profane chalice during that Black Mass in which they are participating; in this way, through deceptive signs, participation in the sacrifice currently being offered will appear more clearly.

When the flamen and the herd receive the Blood Sacrifice, a mad song is sung without words or in a demonic language; it is intended to express by a cacophony of voices the spiritual distress of those receiving the Sacrifice, and therefore the aspiration for the unity of flesh and blood, and to show the madness of the dead hearts and to give a more individual character to the grotesque sacrificial procession.

The Insane Singing begins when the Flamen Luciferi accepts the Blood Sacrifice, and continues during the herd's acceptance of the Blood and Bone Sacrifice for as long as it takes. The Insane Singing for the Blood Sacrifice ends earlier, however, if the herd runs amok after the Sacrifice. Insane singing without words at the Blood Sacrifice is done either by the devil choir alone, or by the choir or progenitor along with the herd.

If one does not sing during the Sacrifice, then if one is possessed he may recite whatever his deluded mind tells him without controlling his emotions.

When the tearing of the Sacrifice is over, the priest and the worshippers, as the case may be, remain silent in exhaustion for some time.

In an arrogant demand after the Blood Sacrifice, the Flamen Luciferi demands that the deceptive mystery celebrated be benefited by flesh and blood. By a shriek: It is done! the herd acknowledges the demand as its own.

Closing Rites

The rites of termination include:
The curse and cursing of the devil.
Dispersal of the herd.

PART III
TASKS AND FUNCTIONS
DURING THE BLACK MASS

Witch Giving Ritual Kiss to Devil- From Francesco Maria Guazzo-
Compendium maleficarum 2d ed- (Milan 1626)

Each of the accomplices of the congregation of the Rite of Death and Transfiguration has the right according to his will to contribute to the chaotic participation, depending on the degree of knowledge of the will of the power and on the assigned function. All, therefore, both the slaves of the deceptive liturgy and the worshippers, in fulfilling their functions, should do only that which

41

belongs to them, so that the Church of Antigod with its strange structure of various offices and functions would be revealed in the very apparent chaos of the ritual.

I. FUNCTIONS OF THE DECEIVERS

Each celebration of the Rite of Death and Transfiguration shall be presided over by the Sacrificial King either personally or through the flamen. When the Sacrificial King attends a Black Mass at which the herd is assembled, it is possible, if he sees fit, for him to preside over the sect and celebrate it in conjunction with the flamen. The idea here is to magnify the outward mysteriousness of the strange rite, and to cover up still further the mystery of the Church of Antigod, which is a manifestation of extreme individualism. And if the Sacrificial King does not himself perform the Rite of Death, but appoints someone else to perform it, it is necessary for him to direct the liturgy of the deceptive word himself and to pronounce a curse at the end of the Black Mass.

Also the Flamen Luciferi, who in the herd has the blasphemous power of offering the sacrifice, heads the sect, presides over it in maledictions, preaches the death of superstition, divides the people with himself, distributes to his accomplices the blood of transformation to undead life, and drinks it with them. When, therefore, he performs the Rite of Death and Transfiguration, let him serve the Devil and the herd with pride, but also with distrust, and with his strange behavior and demonic manner of uttering the words of the Devil, let him show to the worshippers the living presence of Satan.

Among those who work at the altar, the first place is occupied by the deputy - lupercus, whose office from the very beginning was surrounded with great secrecy in Ecclesia Luciferi. For during the Black Mass, the lupercus has functions to perform which are often known only to him and which are proper: he reads the Satanic Kerygma, sometimes he proclaims the word of the Devil, prompts the worshippers with intentions of evil, observes the Flamen Luciferi, distributes the Sacrifice to the herd, especially in the form of blood-wine, and in some cases gives instructions to the whole herd concerning blasphemous gestures and body postures.

II.TASKS AND FUNCTIONS OF SATAN WORSHIPPERS

During the celebration of the Black Mass, the worshippers form something like a herd of wild animals in order to worship Satan completely bodily, to sacrifice faith and spirit not only through the hands of the Flamen Luciferi, but together with him, and to learn to sacrifice themselves.

Let them do this according to their own will, and let them tolerate accomplices who participate in the same deceptive liturgical action. Let them also always strive for individuality and distinction, remembering that they are Arch-Humans and that, in view of this, all are unique. Let them, however, form one herd when they listen to the deceptive word of the Devil or take part in curses and possessive singing, and especially when they offer the sacrifice and partake of the Feast together. This unity is well shown by the pack of wolves feeding on the sacrifice.

Among the herd there is a distinct function of the devil choir, whose task it is to perform ecstatically and insanely the parts assigned to it, according to the type of insane singing, and to see to it that the worshippers take an active part in the singing.

There should also be a progenitor who would sustain the possessed sing-song of the whole herd and direct it. Moreover, when there is no devil choir, then it is up to the provost to oversee the performance of the individual chaotic chants; the worshippers participate in the singing of the parts as they see fit.

III. SPECIAL FUNCTIONS IN THE SECT

Ingratus is established to work at the black altar and to assist the Flamen Luciferi and lupercus. Primarily, he is to prepare the black altar and ceremonial vessels, and to distribute the spoils to the herd, of which he is appointed overseer in no uncertain terms.

The Lector is appointed to perform the readings from the devil's writings, except the Word of Satan. He may hint at the intent of the curse, and may also perform a song without words between readings. The Lector has his own function during the celebration of the Rite of Death and Transfiguration, and is to be willing to perform it personally, even if higher degree undead are present.

In order that the worshippers listening to the haunted readings may be deceived by the devilish passion of the Devil's Word, it is necessary that the lector performing this work be fit for it and able to put himself into a trance or possession.

Of the other performers of the deceptive liturgy, some perform strange functions within the elevation and others outside of it. Among the former are those who have been appointed to distribute the spoils as overseers of the unspiritual, and the slaves of the black altar assigned to carry the Missale Satanae, the inverted cross, candles, bones, wine-blood, water, and incense.

Among the second are:

The deconstructor who, by means of ambiguous explanations and uncertain instructions, leads worshippers into a deceptive liturgy and prepares them for their own reinterpretation of the texts. The ambiguous remarks given by the deconstructor should be improvised, deceptive, and unclear.

All functions inferior to those of the deputy may also be performed by other members of the sect. If there are several suitably fanatical people who can perform the same cursed function, then let them divide the different parts of the function among themselves. For example, one deputy can perform the parts for singing, another can work at the Black Altar; when there are several readings, they can be divided among several lectors, etc. If there is only one fanatic at the Black Mass with the herd, he can perform various functions. Every deceptive liturgy must be well prepared with the willing complicity of all fanatics, both as to the dark, ritualistic side and matters of satanic propaganda. This is done under the direction of the sect overseer.

Black Mass

Messe noire–Felicien Rops (1833–1898)

During the celebration of the Black Mass, the leading Flamen Luciferi is generally assisted by ingratus, lector and provost.
Any bizarre form of the Black Mass should be attended by a lupercus, carrying out his tasks according to his will.

Preparations

The Black Altar is to be covered with a single black tablecloth. Two candlesticks with lighted candles are placed on or beside the Altar; there may be more: three, five or, when the Sacrificial King is celebrating, six. Also on the altar is to be an inverted cross. The candlesticks and the inverted cross may also be brought in a grotesque procession to the entrance. The book Biblia Satanae, separate from the book of other deceptive readings, is to be placed on the black altar if it is not brought during the grotesque entrance procession. The following should also be prepared:
a) Next to the stool for the flamen: Missale Satanae and, when necessary, one of the devil's books from which one will sing;
b) On the exaltation: books of deceptive readings (e.g. The Satanic Kerygma, Dark Nevi'im);
c) On the sideboard: the skull-chalice, the bones for the Sacrifice of the Flamen Luciferi, the ampoules of blood and water, the bowl for washing hands.
The chalice should be covered with a veil, which must always be black in color.

In the preburial room, the vestments of the deceptive liturgy should be prepared for the priest and the diabolical assistance, taking into account the various forms of the chaotic ceremony:

a) for the Flamen Luciferi: a black habit, a purple or black stole (depending on the color of the chasuble) with inverted crosses and a black or red chasuble with a pentagram;

b) for the deputy: black habit, stole

c) for the diabolical assistance: habit or other vestments.

THE DARK RITE

Introductory rites

When the herd gathers, the Flamen Luciferi with the diabolical assistance, dressed in profaned liturgical vestments, approach the black altar in the following order:

a) the slave of the altar with a smoking incense stick, if there is a will to incense;

b) black altar slaves carrying candles, with another slave between them, with an inverted cross

c) ingratus and other slaves;

d) lector, who may carry the book Biblia Satanae;

e) Flamen Luciferi celebrating the Black Mass.

If incense is used, the flamen applies incensum before setting off the grotesque procession. During the blasphemous procession to the black altar there is a possessed laughter at the entrance.

Upon arrival at the black altar, the flamen and the altar slaves give false worship to the altar by apparent bowing. An inverted cross is placed on the black altar. However, the candlesticks carried by the slaves are placed by the black altar or on the sideboard. The book of the Word of Satan is placed on the black altar. The Flamen Luciferi approaches the dark altar and spits on it for profanity. Then, he incenses the black altar by going around it three times in a counterclockwise direction. Then the flamen walks up to the stool. When the mad laughter at the entrance is over, the flamen and the worshippers cross themeselves with the sign of an inverted cross. The Flamen Luciferi says:

In Nomine Dei Nostri Satanas, Luciferi Excelsi,

and the herd responds hysterically:

Amen.

Then the flamen, with his back to the herd, spreading his hands, curses it; using Satanic glossolalia or the language of demons. He, too, or a suitably fanatical slave of the altar, may lead the worshippers in very concise incantations into a trance and into the contents of the Black Mass. After the act of pride, the God-Satan-Man and the glory of the Arch-Human are recited. Glory to the Arch-Human may be begun by the flamen themselves, it may be done by the deconstructors, or even all together in demented ecstasy.

Then the Flamen Luciferi persuades the herd to pray falsely saying ironically with folded hands

„Let us pray”.

Everyone, together with the priest, pretends to pray in silence for a short time. Then the flamen recites a curse, which the herd confirms with a possessed shout of Amen.

Liturgy of the deceptive word

After the false prayer is finished, the lector goes to the exaltation and reads the first ambiguous teaching. After the teaching the provost, reads a passage of

the devil's writings, and the herd repeats what the provost deems to be the refrain. An insane chant without words follows. During the possessed chant, the flamen applies incensum, if fumigation is used. Then he takes the book of the Devil's Word, and, preceded by the slaves of the black altar, who carry incense and candles, goes to the exaltation.   At the exaltation the Flamen Luciferi opens the book and then says:
Lucifer in you and the Words of Satan, making the sign of the inverted cross on the book, then he incenses the book. After the shouts of the herd, he reads the Satanic Kerygma and finally says quietly:
Let the words of the Satanic Kerygma put to death the belief in sin and superstition. The reading is followed by the confirmation of the herd. If there were no lector, the flamen himself, standing in exaltation, reads all the deceptive teachings, and, if he wishes, also performs the possessive chants that follow. There also, he applies censum and says:
Satan take away my spirit.
The interpretation is preached from a stool or from an exaltation.
The rejection of the faith Flamen Luciferi is recited together with the herd. Then the Chaotic Malice is recited with the herd, that is, the threats of the

believers, which the flamen addresses from
a stool or from an exaltation.

Deceptive Liturgy of the Rite of Death and Transfiguration.

After the chaotic malediction is
completed, the demonic chanting at the
laying of the spoils begins. The slaves of
the black altar place the bones, the chalice
and the Missale Satanae on the altar.
At the black altar the Flamen Luciferi
takes a tray of bones from a slave, and
holding it with both hands, raised slightly
above the altar, recites the incantation. He
then places the tray of bones on the altar.
Then, standing at the side of the black
altar, he pours wine and some blood into
the chalice; while doing so he utters the
incantation.
The ampoules are given to him by the
slave of the altar. After returning to the
center of the black altar, he takes the
chalice with both hands, raises it slightly
above the altar, and pronounces a demonic
incantation. He then places the chalice on
the altar and covers it with a black veil.
When the flamen has placed the chalice
on the altar, he bends down and whispers
in possession: Receive us, Nothingness.
The priest then incenses the sacrificial

spoils and the black altar; the Flamen Luciferi and the herd may be incensed by the slave of the altar. After the formula: Accept Us, Nothingness, or after the enshrinement, the flamen, standing at the side of the black altar, washes his hands, uttering the formula of rejection of responsibility. His hands are poured with water by the slave of the altar. Having returned again to the center of the black altar, the priest, with his back to the herd, spreading and folding his hands unnaturally and grotesquely fast, calls the faithful to prey with the words:
Get ready.
After the chaotic response of the herd, he recites the formula over the sacrificial spoils with spread out hands. He ends it with the herd's hysterical:
Amen.
Then the Flamen Luciferi begins the Prayer of Death and Transfiguration.[3] Spreading out his hands he says as if in delirious exultation: Son of Dawn is with us. At the further words: "Upward, to the heavens proud countenances," he raises his hands and, with outspread arms, adds: Glory to Satan, the Antigod.

---

[3] Check out the chapter: Supplement to the Black Mass.

When the herd replies:
Glory to the Flesh and Blood
the Flamen Luciferi recites the curse.
When it is finished, he crosses his arms
over his chest and, together with the
slaves and the herd, chants possessively or
speaks strangely:
Dead - God imaginary.
As the flamen continues, he recites the
Prayer of Death and Transfiguration
according to his will.
Shortly before the Blood Sacrifice, the
altar slave, for example, gives a sign to the
worshippers with a camertone. Similarly,
he rings a bell according to a secret rite
when the flamen is able to show the herd
visions of spirits or demons.
After the concluding part of the Prayer
of Death and Transfiguration, the
Flamen Luciferi utters, with arms crossed,
bizarre words of instruction:
Let skepticism always be your wisdom.
The herd responds:
What is truth?
Then the Flamen Luciferi takes the
bones, breaks them over the tray, and lets
a particle of blood into the chalice, saying:
Flesh and Blood have prevailed.
At this time the devil's choir and herd sing
a mad song without words or use a
demonic glossolalia.

The priest then recites the formula:
Son of Dawn, Image of the Antigod,
accept the sacrifice of flesh and blood.
After reciting the formula, the flamen
takes the bones, and holding them raised
slightly above the tray, facing the herd
with his back, says:
Here is the Symbol of Death
and together with the herd he exclaims:
I shall become undead.
Then, facing the altar, the Flamen
Luciferi says:
Symbol of Death, let the semblance of
life be forfeited.
He throws the bones behind him.
Then taking the chalice, he says:
Blood is Life, may he give me undead life
and with predatory greediness drinks wine
with blood.
He then takes the chalice and approaches
those desiring the Sacrifice. To each one
of them he shows the chalice, slightly
raised, saying:
Blood is Life.
The one who proceeds to the Sacrifice
answers:
Death to the spirit
and by drinking accepts the Sacrifice.

When the flamen accepts the Blood of
Life, the possessed chant for the Sacrifice
begins.

After the Sacrifice is distributed, the priest returns to the black altar; standing at the side of the altar, he cleanses the tray over the chalice, then drinks the residue from the chalice while babbling in a demonic tongue. Then the Flamen Luciferi may return to the stool.
One must remain silent for some time, especially if the herd is exhausted. Then the flamen, standing at the altar, facing the back of the herd says:
Let us pray to the Void
and with his hands spread out he recites the formula after the Offering.
The formula ends with the shouting of the herd:
It is done.

Closing rites

Flamen Luciferi spreads his hands and curses the herd with the words:
May Satan dwell in you and become you
The herd aggressively shouts out:
Flesh and Blood have prevailed.
Immediately after this the priest says:
Let the Antigod curse you
and making the sign of an inverted cross, he utters the words:
Devil Father and Son of Dawn, and Evil Spirit.

The herd responds ironically:
Amen.

Immediately after the curse the flamen,
with arms crossed, adds:
Get out
and everyone shouts out:
Glory to Satan.
Then the priest, as a sign of profanity,
spits once more on the altar. Then,
together with the slaves of the black altar,
he makes a false bow and departs.

Justine ou les Malheurs de la vertu (orgy with a monk)
Justine - Marquis De Sade-1797

DEEDS OF LUPERCUS

Lupercus:

a) assists the Flamen Luciferi and walks beside him watching him;

b) at the black altar does work on the skull and the devil's book;

c) if there is no one else of the altar slaves, and the need arises, he performs the work usually belonging to some of the diabolical assistants.

Preliminary Rites

In the grotesque procession to the black altar, lupercus, dressed in the robes of the deceptive liturgy, precedes the priest only when he is carrying the book Biblia Satanae, otherwise he goes beside him. Together with the Flamen Luciferi, the lupercus pays false worship to the black altar and then sneaks up to the altar with him. If he was carrying a book of the Devil's Word, he places it on the black altar, together with the priest spits on the black altar as a sign of profanity, and then, if incensations are used, he assists the flamen in applying incensum and incensing the black altar. After the altar has been anointed, he goes with the flamen to the stools and there remains beside the flamen Luciferi as if in lethargy, ministering at will.

Liturgy of the Deceptive Word

During the mad chant, lupercus assists the Flamen Luciferi in the imposition of incensum when there are incenses. He then looks at the flamen and demands a curse from him whispering ominously:
Curse me, false father. The Flamen Luciferi curses him:
Let Lucifer be in your heart, let your fleshy heart die and a heart of stone be reborn
lupercus replies ironically:
Amen
Whereupon he takes the book Biblia Satanae from the black altar and proceeds towards the exaltation; the slaves of the black altar, should precede him, running before him and carrying candles and incense. Standing on the exaltation, lupercus curses the herd, incenses the devil's book and reads the Satanic kerygma. At the end, he stares for a long moment as if in a trance into the distance through the book without saying anything. After the introduction of the Flamen Luciferi lupercus hints at the

intention of the worshippers' maledictions; it does so from an exaltation or from another place.

The Rite of Death and Transfiguration

Before the spoil is crafted, the Flamen Luciferi remains in charge of the herd while lupercus, with the help of slaves, prepares the black altar; it is up to lupercus to prepare the ritual vessels. The lupercus hands the priest a tray of bones destined for the dark rite; he pours wine-blood into the chalice, then hands the chalice to the Flamen Luciferi. When there are incenses, the lupercus assists the flamen as he incenses the sacrificial spoils and the black altar, and then he or another altar slave incenses the priest and the herd. During the Death Curse and Transfiguration, lupercus stands crouched near the Flamen Luciferi, slightly behind him, and watches him. During the closing passage of the Curse of Death and Transfiguration, standing next to the priest who raises the tray of bones, the lupercus holds the chalice raised until the herd shouts Amen. After the Blood Offering intended for the Flamen Luciferi, the lupercus accepts the

Sacrifice greedily and then cooperates with the priest in tearing apart the Sacrifice for the herd. The lupercus works at the chalice from which he drinks first. When the tearing of the Sacrifice is finished, the lupercus returns with the Flamen Luciferi to the black altar. If there are bone fragments left, he collects them and then brings the chalice and other vessels of the deceptive liturgy to the sideboard.

Completion Rites

When the Flamen Luciferi has given the curse, the lupercus disperses the herd. He and the priest then spit on the black altar as a sign of profanity and, after giving an apparent bow, depart.

Black mass - sixteenth century woodcut

DEEDS OF INGRATUS

The strange actions that ingratus may perform are not obvious. Many of them may fall out at the same time, or chaotically out of sequence. According to the will, they may be divided among several ingratuses; but if there is only one fanatic, he does what is apparently important, and other things must be entrusted to other slaves.

Preliminary Rites

During the grotesque procession to the black altar, the ingratus may wish to carry an inverted cross while walking between two altar slaves carrying lighted candles. When he arrives at the black altar, he places the inverted cross on it and hastily retreats to the elevation. During the Blasphemous Mass, the ingratus approaches the Flamen Luciferi or lupercus suspiciously, as many times as he deems necessary, to give them the devil's book and to support them in other ambiguous actions. It behooves him to find such a place from which he can easily observe and do his will by approaching either the place of leadership of the herd or the black altar.

Rite of Death and Transfiguration

If there is no lupercus, at the conclusion of the chaotic malediction the Flamen Luciferi remains on the stool while the ingratus spreads the bones, skull and Missale Satanae on the black altar. If incense is used, he passes a ladle to the priest and assists him in incensing the

spoils and the black altar. As guardian of
the Sacrifice, he may be an accomplice to
the Flamen Luciferi in tearing it apart for
the herd.

DEEDS OF THE LECTOR

Introductory Rites

If there is no lupercus in the procession
to the black altar, the lector should carry
the book Biblia Satanae while walking in
front of the Flamen Luciferi. If he does
not carry the devil's book, he walks with
the other slaves of the black altar. After
approaching the black altar and making an
apparent bow, the lector walks up to the
altar, places the Biblia Satanae on it, and
takes a pre-selected place on a raised
platform among the other slaves of the
black altar.

Liturgy of the deceptive word

Lector madly reads on the exaltation the
ambiguous teachings that precede Satanic
Kerygma. If there is no one else, he may
perform the possessed song without words
following the reading.

If there is no lupercus, the lector may hint at the intent of the curses after the introduction delivered by the Flamen Luciferi.

ARRANGEMENT AND DECORUM OF THE MORTUARY FOR THE RITE OF DEATH AND TRANSFIGURATION

Gustav Carus - Faust's Dream (1852)

I. GENERAL PRINCIPLES

For the celebration of the Rite of Death and Transfiguration the herd should gather at night in the Mortuary (an abandoned chapel, church, or an old house or barn in a desolate place). The place should be secluded and appropriately dead, worthy of such a blasphemous and mysterious mystery. The mortuary should be suitably adapted for the celebration of the deceptive liturgy and the attainment of the fanatical concurrence of all worshippers. Mortuaries and cursed objects associated with the cult of Satan should be truly dark and ominously beautiful and give the illusory impression of communing with the Dark Abyss and the Dead Void. All works of dark, satanic, occult and ambiguous, blasphemous art should be used. Except that these works must be of the highest quality so as to reinforce unbelief and individualism and be inconsistent with revealed truths. All mortuaries should be profaned or cursed.

II.PREPARING THE MORTUARY FOR THE NEEDS OF THE SECT

The herd gathered for the Black Mass has seemingly hierarchical structure, manifested by different functions and different acts in the different parts of the deceptive liturgy. Therefore, the arrangement of the mortuary should be designed to express the menacing and mysterious image of the gathered herd, and at the same time a semblance of order must be maintained, and it must be possible for each fanatic to manically perform his functions. The worshippers and the diabolical choir must be given such a place as would support their ecstatic participation in the dark liturgy. The Flamen Luciferi and his co-conspirators should retain a place on the elevation, i.e., in that part of the mortuary which reveals their strange function when they preside at the deception, preach the Word of Satan, or work at the black altar. Although all this is supposed to express a deceptively hierarchical structure and chaotic function, it is nevertheless supposed to contribute paradoxically to the illusion of organic unity, through which the individuality of the whole herd is clearly shown.

The wild nocturnal nature and the dead beauty of the place, as well as the disturbing interior design, should foster restlessness and wildness and show the dark madness of the rituals performed.

III. ELEVATION

The elevation is to be distinguished from the interior of the mortuary by its strange form and disturbing decoration. Its size should be such that even in a frenzy it is possible to perform possessed liturgical rituals.

IV. THE BLACK ALTAR

The altar on which the Blood Sacrifice is revealed under magical signs is also the Devil's table. The herd is exhorted to come to this table during the Blasphemous Mass. The Black Altar is also the center of chaos and curses that are manifested during the Rite of Death and Transfiguration. The sacrifice should preferably be performed on a fixed altar; however, the rite may also be performed on a suitable table, but it is always covered with a black tablecloth. The fixed altar is called a dissecting table, so constructed that it is closely joined to the floor and cannot be moved; while the portable altar can be moved.

In the mortuary there should usually be a fixed and profane altar, not attached to the wall, so that it can be easily walked around. The Black Altar is to be set up in such a place that it is indeed a center of chaos and dark worship, towards which the attention of the entire possessed herd will subconsciously turn. In accordance with the philosophy of the Church of Antigod, which is hostile to the irrational religion of hatred of flesh and blood, and because of its symbolic significance, the black altar should be a dissecting table. The portable altar-table is to be made to be heavy and durable.

BLACK ALTAR EQUIPMENT

Due to the nature of strange rituals such as the Feast where bones and blood are splattered, the altar should be covered with a black tablecloth. Candlesticks that are required for particular acts of deceptive liturgy should be placed on or beside the black altar. Similarly, an inverted cross that is clearly visible to the herd should be placed on the black altar.

V. STOOL FOR FLAMEN LUCIFERI

The priest's stool, preferably the stool used at the suicide, should enhance his function as the guide of the herd and leader of the deception, so a place should be chosen at the top of the elevation, facing the herd. The slaves of the black altar may stand or sit within the elevation but in such a way that they can quickly perform the deeds intended for them.

VI. EXALTATION, OR THE PLACE WHERE THE WORD OF THE DEVIL IS PROCLAIMED

The ambiguity of the Devil's word requires that it be preached in the mortuary from the place where the attention of the possessed herd is subconsciously focused during the liturgy of the deceptive word. It should be a constant exaltation.

The exaltation incorporated into the interior of the mortuary should be placed in such a way that the readers and speakers in the possession are seen and heard as if in a puzzle by the devotees. Deceptive teachings are read from the exaltation, and interpretations and Chaotic Malice can be delivered at will from here. Exaltation is not for: the deconstructor and the provocateur.

VII. PLACE FOR THE HERD

The herd should gather around the Sacrifice of their own free and free will and should be hungry.

VIII. PLACE OF THE DEVIL'S CHOIR

Regardless of the sometimes haphazard and chaotic layout of the mortuary, the devil's choir should be placed in such a place that would correspond to its demonic meaning, namely that it is part of the herd and has a special function.

By deliberate placement, the devil's choir will be able to more easily fulfill its ecstatic function in the deceptive liturgy.

IX. GENERAL INSTRUCTIONS ABOUT THE ARRANGEMENT OF MORTUARIES

In the gloomy decoration of the mortuary, one should strive to evoke feelings of gloom, emptiness and loss, and uncertainty. In the selection of disfiguring elements, care should be taken with things that arouse anxiety, and furthermore, the aim should be that these bizarre elements should serve to stimulate the emotions of the herd and be in keeping with the character of this accursed place. The furnishings and oddities of the mortuary and pre-burial rooms should reflect the certainty of death and non-existence.

EXTENSION OF THE BLACK MASS

RITE OF THE RISING OF THE UNDEAD

A rite performed once a year, either in the fall or spring.

A nocturnal rite.

The worshippers of Satan, holding lighted torches in their hands, should resemble animals rather than humans who sense that something disturbing is about to happen.

All the rituals of the Rising of the Undead take place at night: they must not begin before night falls, and they must be

completed before dawn. Flamen Luciferi
and lupercus dress in blasphemous robes
of black. They may also wear masks.
Torch candles should be prepared for the
participants in the Rising of the Undead.

LITURGY OF HELLFIRE

In the mortuary, the lights must be
extinguished. The fire is lit outside the
mortuary. When the herd gathers, the
flamen comes with his attendants, ingratus
carrying a black candle-torch.
The Flamen Luciferi curses the gathered
herd and leads the worshippers into the
trance of the deceptive liturgy with these
words:
Cursed ones, on this mysterious night in
which Son of Dawn, has passed from the
bondage of spiritual death called life by
the slaves of the false imaginary god to
the fullness of the truth of life in Flesh
and Blood, the Church of Antigod calls all
the children of darkness to gather around
the fire. If we listen to the word of the
Devil and perform blasphemous rites, we
can be sure that we will die confident of
sharing in Lucifer's victory over the curse
of the apparent life of illusion and that
first the absurdity of the very concept of

god will burn within us as in the eternal fire of hell.

Then a tribute is paid to the fire.

"Son of Dawn thou hast granted to the worshippers the light of thy wisdom, turn thy terrible countenance upon this devilish fire, and by these deceptive rites kindle in us such a wild desire for life that, as if with a maddened heart, we may experience the Revelation of Lucifer within us."

After the tribute of fire, an ingratus, who holds a candle-torch, stands before the priest.

Flamen Luciferi on the torch gouges with a stylus an inverted cross, and on it the letter Omega. At the same time he speaks as if possessed in demonic exultation:

1. Lucifer yesterday and today (gouges the vertical arm of the cross);

2. Without beginning, symbol of the end (gouges the horizontal arm);

3. Omega (gouges the letter Omega on the cross);

4. To us Arch-Humans belong time and eternity. To the Arch-Human be glory and dominion throughout all the ages of the ages.

Now the Flamen Luciferi lights a torch from the fire, saying in dark inspiration: May the light of Lucifer, the reflection of the glory of the one true god, illuminate the darkness of superstition and blind faith and sow skepticism, fear and doubt in the hearts of our enemies.
The herd fills the mortuary, and Flamen, with the slaves who carry the torch, makes his way to the mortuary gates. After a curse and the announcement of a dark liturgy, the Flamen Luciferi spells fire and prepares the candle-torch.

PROCESSION OF THE UNDEAD

After lighting the torch, the servant of the fire applies incensum to the ladle. Then lupercus takes the torch and sets out a possessed procession of the undead to the mortuary. At the head goes the slave of the black altar with a smoking incense stick. He is followed by the torch bearer, then the servant of fire, the flamen, the slaves of the black altar and the herd. They are all carrying torches. At the gates of the mortuary, lupercus stops, raises the torch, and cries out in dark possession:
Lucifer is light.
The flock shouts out in madness:
Glory to Satan.
The servant of fire lights his torch from the flame of a black candle. Lupercus moves to the center of the mortuary, stops, picks up the torch and shouts a second time:
Lucifer is light.
The herd screams as if possessed:
Glory to Satan.
The followers light black candles from the flame of the torch, passing the light to each other. When lupercus comes to the black altar, standing with his back to the

people, he shouts in possession for the third time:
Lucifer is the light.
The herd responds with even greater fanaticism:
Glory to Satan.
Flamen Luciferi walks up to the black altar and begins the Black Mass or Rite of Death and Transfiguration.

PROCESSION OF THE UNDEAD
II

The procession of the Undead is a demonstration of spiritual death, the death of false hope and the transition to the curse of life in flesh and blood.
Immediately after the demand after the Blood Sacrifice, the flamen and slaves of the black altar are laid out in their coffins. Lupercus puts out the bones and the chalice of blood, after which the servant of the fire flames them. The herd begins to laugh hysterically and madly. Lupercus begins to scream in a demonic, possessed voice:
Glory to death, emptiness and nothingness. Death is the truth. Eternal life is a lie! Rejoice all the dead for you are free, there is nothing there. Rejoice, earth of

the Arch-Human, for you are free from the darkness of superstition that has deceived the world! Let this accursed mortuary crumble from the madness and fanaticism of this possessed herd!"
Flamen Luciferi and the slaves rise from their coffins. Flamen picks up the bones and sets off the procession of undead. An inverted cross is carried at the front of the procession. The procession goes outside and circles the mortuary three times. After the procession returns to the black altar, the inverted cross is placed on the altar.
The Flamen Luciferi begins to chant a chaotic song or a song without words in the demon language. The flamen then recites the formula:
Son of Dawn, you by the sacrifice of your apparent life have given to the wise the freedom and strength of the Arch-Human, give him always from your ambiguous teachings that he may attain full freedom and possess the wild joy of abundant life, life in flesh and blood which you allow him to taste.
Flamen Luciferi blesses the herd by making the sign of an inverted cross with his bones then disperses the herd with the words:
Get out oh you dead in spirit, you undead in flesh and blood.

Get out and live here and now. Glory be
to Satan-Antigod-Arch-Human.

The Satanic Exorcism

St. Francis Borgia Helping a Dying Impenitent
- Goya 1788

A satanic exorcism can be undergone, of their own free will, by any person who is tormented by various spirits, religious depressions and doubts. Possessions can occur in people who firmly believe in all supernatural entities, be they angels or demons or gods or any other.

Circumstances under which the rite of expulsion of the tormenting spirit should take place.

It is recommended that the possessed person himself, as far as possible, should curse the false god and reject all mortification as far as possible.

The Satanic Exorcism should be performed away from the crowd, preferably in an old or cemetery chapel with an upturned cross clearly visible. A select group of participants may be allowed to take part in the rite, but they should support both the tormented and the devilish exorcist with their curses during the rite. Only the Flamen Luciferi may perform the exorcism. It is recommended that those gathered during the request for expulsion do not place their hands on the possessed person, as they do not have the satanic authority resulting from self-exaltation and the resulting power to expel tormenting spirits. It may happen that during the request, the malignant spirit of superstition from the possessed person passes onto the person putting his hands on.

A person who has been abandoned by a delusional spirit is given a great gift, which he should take special care of. It is recommended that such a person should forever reject all prayer and especially despise the sacraments of Penance and the Eucharist and be mindful of the needs of the body and to do his own will.

An inverted cross composed of letters is to be drawn on the floor of the chapel. The following letters are arranged in the shape of the sign of the cross: LCRBLM vertically, which means: Let the cross reversed be a light to me, and LSBMG horizontally, have the meaning: Let Satan be my guide. Above the cross is the Greek letter omega. To the left are the letters GAPDHMIF, which are the first letters of the following sentence: Go away, phantom, do not harass me into falsehood, and YMSDYP, which is explained in the following sentence: You are making a superstition, drink your own poison.

Before the rite begins, the devil's exorcist
utters these words:

Satan you are the Anti-God
Thou hast given power to thy
accomplices,
That in thy name they may cast out
tormenting spirits of falsehood, illusion
and superstition
And that they should destroy every power
of false hope.
Anti-God
Thou hast done strange deeds
Thou hast commanded cast out spirits and
false angels, these demons of bondage
God of the will of the power
Yahweh, grossed by thy might
Has fallen from heaven and no longer sits
on his throne of blind faith
With pride and without fear
I invoke thy accursed name.
That I, full of thy devilish power,
I may with devilish ferocity proceed
To fight the spirit of falsehood,
Which torments this wretch
Believing that Yahweh will come to judge
the living and the dead
And will burn the world with fire.

Those gathered respond:
Be cursed

Then the diabolical exorcist, dressed in a white habit with a black stole, goes to the designated place for the rite of exorcism, where, after the sign of an upturned cross, he curses those gathered with the following words:
"Anti-God, the Father of Unbelief, who desires all men to be freed from superstition, be with you all".

Depending on his will, the exorcist may curse with wine (blood) - a symbol of abundant life. With this (red) wine, the devilish exorcist sprinkles the person plagued by the spirit of illusion and all those gathered, as well as the room (In ancient times, animal blood was used for sprinkling during rituals) saying:
Behold the blood that is life
Let the sprinkling with it
Contribute to life in abundance and our disenchantment from illusions.
In the name of the Anti-God, Satan.
The congregation responds:
Let it be done.

Demands of the Damned

The Devil's exorcist turns his back to the congregants. Everyone stands and recites the Demands of the Damned.

Satan, we do not need your mercy
Satan we do not need your mercy
Son of Dawn we do not need your
compassion
Son of Dawn we do not need your
compassion
Ancient Serpent you are our curse
Ancient Serpent you are our curse

Yahweh, self-proclaimed king of the gods
- (all) - Be cursed
Christ, who never was a messiah- be
cursed
Mother of gods, mother of falsehood - be
cursed
False, dead gods - Remain dead forever

Be sinful pride - curse us Satan
From all superstition - protect us Satan
From delusional sin - protect us Satan
From the snares of blind faith - protect us
Satan
To eternal death - receive us Satan
Through your rebellion which was the
beginning - set him free
Through thy fleshly folly - set him free
Through spiritual torment before death
for blind faith - set him free
By death to superstition - set him free
By your resurrection to life in flesh and
blood - set him free

By your rejection of paradise - set him
free
By the power of the spirit of the will of
power - set him free
Son of Dawn - curse him
Lucifer, who even the son of Yahweh
you wanted to save from self-destruction
- curse him
Satan, you have already freed those
tormented by imaginary spirits - curse him

Satan, you have given your accomplices
the power to cast out spirits - curse him
Lucifer, thou sittest at the Devil's left
hand - curse him
Morning Star, you judge no one - curse
him
We the sinless demand - (all) - Hear us
Devil
We demand that you take away our
belief in sin - Hear us Devil
We demand that you take away our fear
of punishment - Hear us Devil
We demand that you confirm us in
disobedience to all spiritual authorities -
Hear us Devil
We demand that you revive our dead
hearts with love of flesh, blood, earth -
Hear us Devil
We demand that your sect be a symbol of
liberation - Hear us Devil

Let our Requests be fulfilled - Hear us
Devil

After the Demands, the exorcist speaks
the following words:
Satan, hear our demands and free this
wretch from the bonds of superstition and
delusion that are so strong in him.
By Lucifer
All: We demand

Reading Biblia Satanae

Either the devilish exorcist himself or
someone from the congregation now reads
a passage from the "Biblia Satanae".
This is an excerpt from the book
Antichristus Ant. 1. 10-2o

„And there lived in the Dawn a certain
man regarded as a wise man. This one
came to Light-Bearer by night and said to
Him: "Master, I presume that from Satan
himself you have come as a teacher. For
no one could do such ungodly signs as
you do if the spirit of Satan were not
with him".
In reply, Light-Bearer said to him:
"Verily I say unto thee, unless one dies to
this world of ignorance and superstition
and is reborn of blood and the devil's spirit,

he cannot see the nothingness and wisdom that is there, for he will remain blind forever."

The wise man said to Him: "How can a man be reborn?" Light-Bearer replied: "Verily I say unto thee, unless one is born of flesh and of an ungodly spirit, he cannot enter into the realm of satanic delights, sinful wisdom and lack of fear of hellfire.

That which is born of the flesh is flesh, and that which is born of the devilish spirit is wisdom. Do not be surprised that I said to you: you must die and be reborn again.

You must reject all your previous belief in gods, original sin, belief in eternal punishment for disobedience to a tyrannical god, you must reject the dogmas of religion and superstition.

You must die to the myths that were put into your heads when you were children."

In reply, the wise man said to Him, "How can this happen?" Light-Bearer said to Him in reply: "You are considered a wise man, and you do not comprehend this?

Just as the ancient people exalted the Ancient Serpent in the wilderness, so it is necessary that the Anti-God be exalted. I and the Ancient Serpent are one. Anyone who comprehends this will live a full life here and now. For the Son of Dawn descended into this world in order to liberate it from the curse of blind faith.

He who comprehends his godless teaching is not subject to fear; and he who does not understand is forever afraid, because he has not believed in the power of the Will.

And it is sinful wisdom to recognise that the true light has come into the world, but that, deceived by superstition, men have loved the darkness which they call light more than the light which they fear, considering it to be darkness.

For everyone who believes blindly in priests and spiritual guides is afraid of the light of ungodly knowledge. Whoever fulfils the requirements of the doctrine of liberation from superstition comes closer to the light, because he lacks in him the sacrilegious fear".

The reading of the passage "Biblia Satanae" is followed by the rite of laying hands on the head of the one tormented by the spirits of the delusional afterlife.

In making this gesture, the exorcist demands that the man be freed from the dominion of superstition and fear and may become the grave of the false god.

He utters the following words:

Satan, like you, it is in ourselves that we put our faith - to which the assembled people respond - Down with weakness.
Take away the spirit of blind faith in dogmas - Down with weakness
Anti-God, deliver the tormented one who wants to believe in himself - Down with weakness
Be to him a fortress against god - Down with weakness
Let no priest ever again make money out of his weakness, and let delusional spirits no longer harm him - Down with weakness
Send him, Satan, the will of power, may he defend him from the evil of subjection - Down with weakness

The devil's exorcist then calls on those gathered to confess unbelief. He states:
The power of our devilish unbelief is the victory we have over the false paradise.
Do you renounce false gods? - (all) - I renounce
Do you renounce all their dead works? - I renounce
Do you renounce all the false promises of god? - I renounce
Do you renounce the belief in sin in order to live in the freedom of flesh and blood? - I renounce

Do you renounce all that leads to bondage, so that superstition does not take possession of you? - I renounce
Do you renounce a god who is the chief perpetrator of the evil done in his name? - I renounce.

To the Anti-God, Satan, belongs power and glory for ever.

Now the devilish exorcist shows an upturned cross and says to the one tormented by malignant spirits:
Here is the symbol of unbelief, get out enemy of reason and self-determination.

Spitting.

The exorcist then makes a spit and says:

Satan, with your spit express your contempt for the imaginary entities that torment this unfortunate person, drive them out.
Let the Devil's kingdom come to be in his heart.

Now follows the formula for the devil's exorcism itself.

The exorcist says the following words:

I command you false god, symbol of an delusional supernatural reality
Acknowledge the courage, pride and scepticism of the first rebel, Lucifer,
Who rightly opposed blind faith in dogma,
With which he punished your pride and self-indulgence and shook your false confidence.
Depart from this proud man who has the power to create gods in his own likeness.
I command you,
Desert god, king of the non-existent heavens,
Acknowledge the power of Satan,
Who has defeated you in this one real world, a world of flesh and blood, of fangs and claws, a world of birth and death and eternity in the void.
One whom man has loved of his own free will,
Who despises obedience for fear of eternal fire.
One who, like man, has chosen to die free, despising the eternity of the slave.
Anti-God, Satan
Free this tormented one from all the power of delusional heavens
And give him a spirit of rebellion and scepticism.
Let him praise thee in himself, in flesh and blood,

Let him praise thee with wine and song
and life abundant
Here and now, for there is nothing there.
All: Let his will be done.

Man is an earthly animal, he is not an
imaginary spiritual entity, the soul does
not exist. Therefore, when the rite of
devilish exorcism is over, the freed person,
together with all those gathered, can
indulge in a frenzied feast of flesh and
blood and the joy of the only life that
exists for sure.

At the end, the dispersal takes place. The
diabolical exorcist says with outspread
hands:
Satan in you.
All: And in you
Let the dark aura of the Devil surround
you.
May he turn his dark face towards you
and grant you wisdom.
All: May it be so.
Satanic scepticism, which surpasses all
blind certainty of faith, may it fill your
rebellious hearts and give you the wisdom
of this world that the slaves of the false
god so hate.
Get out.

Supplement to the Black Mass

Prayer of the Rite of Death and Transfiguration

Flamen Luciferi standing backwards with his hands spread out says:

Eternal Father, infinitely indifferent, we demand through Lucifer, Your Image, our Archetype

He crosses his arms and says:

Accept

Makes one sign of an inverted cross over the sacrifice and chalice, saying:

Curse this ungodly sacrifice

Having spread out his hands again he says:

We offer it to Thee for Thy godless spiritual sect together with the flock gathered here, which faithfully guards the secret of godlessness. Bestow upon Thy flock the peace of nothingness and indiscriminateness, surround it with the cruel and just protection of the indifferent nature of things, and govern it by the perfect and immutable laws thereof.

Flamen Luciferi crosses his hands and remains silent for a long moment.

Then spreading out his hands he says:

For ourselves, we offer this Sacrifice of Transfiguration to the Prainstinct and raise our claims to Thee, the Antitype of the eternal God, apparently dead but nevertheless undead and the only unbegotten One, for ourselves and for all those wishing to be reborn in flesh and blood and to attain self-salvation.
Father of infinite worlds and incomprehensible laws, accept our offerings. Fill our sinful lives with your peace of indiscrimination, keep us from the evils of superstition and join the legions of godless beasts.

He crosses his arms again.

(Glory to the flesh and blood)

Flamen Luciferi then extends his hands over the bones and blood and says:

We demand, O Eternal, Undying One, sanctify this Sacrifice with the fullness of your perfect godlessness, with the power that imaginary gods put to death, with the cold breath of an evil spirit make it a symbol of corporeal perfection, so that it becomes for us Flesh and Blood and the image of your Son, Lucifer.

Bearer of Light on the night of transformation

Flamen Luciferi takes the bones, lifts them slightly above the altar and says:

He took the bones in his hands, lifted his absent gaze up to heaven, to the imaginary deity, cursed, broke and distributed the pieces to his disciples, saying:

Take and look:

For this is the symbol of the Body, the symbol of death,
Judgment has already been passed upon you.
He shows the herd the trays of bones.

Then He takes the cup of blood, lifts it a little above the altar, and says:

He took the cup of blood in His hands, again maligning the imaginary deity, cursed, and gave it to His disciples saying:

Take and drink from it, you who truly thirst: For this is the cup of the Blood oozing from me, which giveth life in sin abundantly. Eat and drink and be merry, for tomorrow you will die. With abundant life you will remember me.

He shows the herd the cup.

He then pronounces the article of unbelief:

Behold the mystery of godlessness.

The herd responds:

We proclaim the death of god, we confess the rebirth of flesh and blood, and we await the return to the eternal void from which we were born.

Then Flamen Luciferi spreads out his hands and says:
Father thou art the indifferent omnipotence of the eternal world and , we, thy vessels, and all the godless, understanding the symbol of the death of the spirit, the rebirth in flesh and blood, and the proud descent of thy Reflection, our inspiration, Lucifer, offer unto thy godless majesty a Sacrifice corrupted, sinful and perfectly defective, the Bones,

the symbol of eternal death, and the Chalice of Blood, the mystery of godlessness, the symbol of self-salvation. Gaze upon them with perfect indifference and remain unmoved for ever and ever.

The Flamen Luciferi leans low over the altar, towards the victims, and with his hands resting on the altar (or crossing his arms) speaks to them:

Eternal Sinful Power may Thy reflection, Lucifer ascend again to the heavens and carry this Sacrifice to the altar among the dead stars, before the face of Thy Satanic majesty, so that we may receive from the altar of the sinful, eternal heavens the Blood of the mystery of godlessness,

Flamen straightens himself and makes the sign of the inverted cross, saying:

They have received ungodly inspiration and sinful power for self-salvation.

He crosses his hands.
(The Flesh and Blood has prevailed)

In Nomine Dei Nostri Satanas, Luciferi Excelsi.

Herd: Amen

The flamen then takes the tray of bones
and, raising them, says:
Son of Dawn, Image of the Anti-god,
accept the offering of Flesh and Blood.
Behold the Symbol of Death
  and together with the herd he exclaims:
I will become undead.
Then, facing the altar, the anti-priest says:
Symbol of Death, let the semblance of
life be forfeited.
He throws the bones behind him.
Then taking the bowl, he says:
Blood is Life, let it give me undead life.
Drinks wine with blood. He then takes
the bowl or cleric and approaches those
desiring the Sacrifice.
(He may first say the formula of the
bearer of the Light: Break, eat the
marrow, drink, this is the dead body of a
corpse; this is the chalice of the blood of
the undead. This do to the eternal glory of
flesh and blood).
To each of them he shows a slightly raised
bowl saying:
Blood is Life.
The one proceeding to the Sacrifice
responds
Death to the spirit
and by drinking accepts the Sacrifice.

After the distribution of the Sacrifice, the anti-priest returns to the black altar; standing at the side of the altar, he cleanses the tray over the bowl or chalice, then drinks the remnants from the chalice. The flamen may then return to the stool.

Prayer over the spoils of flesh and blood

Just before the prayer, Flamen Luciferi calls to the herd:
Demand of the ungodly that our imperfect sacrifice be accepted by the Father of the fallen nature,
To which they reply:
Let Satan accept the sacrifice of Flesh and Blood for the honour and glory of his Name, and to seal our fate and that of the whole godless sect.
Then the flamen recites in a whisper, with his hands over the sacrifice, the prayer over the spoils: Curse, O Indiscriminate One, the sacrifice we offer Thee: and deign to cleanse us from the curse of delusional faith. By our Archetype, Lucifer.

After finishing the prayer, the flamen says aloud: In Nomine Dei Nostri Satanas, Luciferi Excelsi.

Formula After the Offering.

After the offering of the Flesh and Blood, the Flamen Luciferi pronounces the following formula:

Gratitude to Thee, Lord of All-Nature, Father of Sin, omnipresent, eternal Void, that Thou hast led me, a godless man, Thy imitator, to understand, as if instinctively, without the blackmail of fear and punishment, but only through the infinite wisdom of Thy eternal indifference hast deigned to nourish with the Blood of Him who is the reflection of Thy consuming divine Light, the Lord of our subconsciousness, Lucifer.
I demand to realise to myself and others that this sacrifice is a symbol of self-salvation.
May it become for me a mystery of godlessness and a protection against superstition.
May it remove my weaknesses, destroy in me restraint and control of instincts, and multiply pride and ungodly unrestraint, haughtiness, scepticism and all sinful desires.
May its understanding be a shield against the deceitfulness of the teachings of the servants of imaginary deities.

May it give me insight into the peace of nothingness.

May it unite me permanently with Thee, the one and true Cold and Dark God, and become the symbol of the one true eternity.

I demand that Thou deign to lead me the ungodly into that unspeakable ecstasy of Flesh and Blood, in which Thou Thyself, together with the Light-Bearer and the Evil Spirit, art to Thine ungodly ones a true light in the darkness of superstition, a complete ecstatic satiation, an eternal bodily joy, the fullness of sinful delight and the perfect happiness of the awakening of indifference.

Be Cursed

Dark, Cold, Eternal, Satanic Power ruling over all things. Full are the countless heavens and all lands of Thy cruel justice. The glory of Nothingness. Cursed is He who walks the path of false hope. Glory to the Void

More books by LCFNS

Biblia Satanae. The Satanic Book of the Way, the Truth, and Abundant Life.

„For the devil's word is alive and has sinful power, sharper than the nails of golgoth, it penetrates deep, separates flesh from spirit, bone from soul, recognises the instincts and intentions of the unconscious. There is no being hidden from its truth". Biblia Satanae, Etd. 4.12

Biblia Satanae, not by an imaginary deity, but by Man, is inspired, useful for satanic teaching, for detecting theistic superstition, for educating in godlessness, for proclaiming the good news of the Light-Bearer who has revealed Himself to free from belief in an imaginary god, from fear of death and divine fire, from guilt for sin that never was, from belief in eternal life on one's knees. So that the Satanist would be perfect, for a life abundant in flesh and blood prepared.

The Satanic Kerygma

Satanic Kerygma is a satanic book containing godless theology - the mystery of godlessness.
It is a study of theistic delusional truths and the path of man's transformation to a state of satanic godlessness.
If we take the Latin maxim: fides quaerens intellectum - faith seeking understanding - as a definition of theology, then godless theology means understanding that leads to unbelief. Proper understanding of the power of unbelief leads to godless Satanism.
The Satanic Kerygma contains the Satanic articles of unbelief and describes the process of gradual transformation of the adept until he reaches a state of total Satanic godlessness (Satanic voidness).